NATIONAL GEOGRAPHIC

Ladders

Pacific COAST
WHERE ON EARTH?

EXPLORING THE PACIFIC COAST

by Brett Gover

Sunny beaches and giant redwoods. **Glaciers**—large sheets of ice—and **volcanoes**. The Pacific coast has it all.

This region borders the Pacific Ocean and spans several thousand miles. It includes Alaska, Washington, Oregon, and California. The Pacific coast also includes the main islands of Hawaii. Hawaii lies more than 2,000 miles from California, in the middle of the ocean.

Most major **earthquakes** and volcanic eruptions in the United States occur along the Pacific coast. An earthquake is a violent shaking of Earth's surface. A volcano is an opening in Earth's crust where melted rock and gases escape from underground. Still, many people live here. The same **geological** forces that cause earthquakes also create beautiful landscapes.

Many people go whale and dolphin watching along the Pacific coast. They will see sights like this humpback whale back-flipping into the water. When a whale jumps out of the water it is called breaching.

Where on Earth?

THE PACIFIC COAST

Check out these facts about the five states along the Pacific coast.

California

Redwood trees in California are the world's tallest trees. The tallest redwood soars to about 365 feet. That's the height of a 30-story building!

Alaska

The northern lights can be seen in the night sky of Alaska. They form when tiny bits of matter sent from the sun hit the gases in Earth's atmosphere.

Hawaii

The Hawaiian Islands are actually the tops of volcanoes. They rise from the ocean floor. Mauna Loa is the world's largest volcano. Kilauea has been erupting since 1983.

Alaska

Hawaii

Washington

Washington's official state gem is petrified wood. That's wood that has turned into stone. Dead trees fell and were buried under dirt and rock. Over millions of years, minerals replaced the wood and it became a fossil.

Washington

Oregon

California

Oregon

Sea lions and whales gather at Sea Lion Cave in Florence, Oregon. Can you tell the difference between a sea lion and a seal? Part of a sea lion's ear is on the outside of its body. A seal does not have visible ears.

Check In What are some things that all five states along the Pacific coast have in common?

5

THE RING OF FIRE

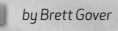

by Brett Gover

You're in your room when you hear a rumbling sound. It grows louder. The floor begins to shake. A vase topples over. You try to stand, but the shaking knocks you off balance. A few seconds later, the shaking stops. You have just experienced an earthquake.

Earthquakes happen almost daily on the Pacific coast. Most of them are too small to feel, though. The Pacific coast is part of the Ring of Fire, an area of land about 25,000 miles long. In the Ring of Fire, the earth shakes and volcanoes explode regularly. Most of the world's earthquakes and volcanic eruptions happen there.

< In March 2009, Alaska's ice-covered Mount Redoubt erupted. A column of ash shot more than 10 miles up into the sky. The eruption lasted for two weeks.

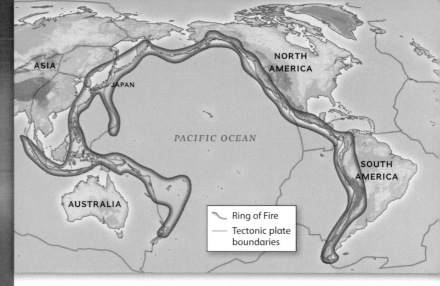

∧ The Ring of Fire follows the coastline of the Pacific Ocean. Read about Earth's plates on the next page.

EARTH IN MOTION

What causes these earthquakes and volcanic eruptions? Earth's outer layer, or crust, is made up of pieces called **plates**. These plates meet deep underground. On Earth's surface, large cracks called **faults** can form. Faults show us where the plates meet.

The plates move only a few inches each year. As a plate moves, its edge pushes against another plate. As one plate sinks beneath the other, heat underground melts the lower plate. This melting forms molten, or hot, rock. The molten rock rises toward Earth's surface. If it reaches the surface it can erupt, forming a volcano.

⌃ **Carrizo Plain, California** The San Andreas Fault is where the Pacific and North American plates meet. It is about 800 miles long. When it shifts, it causes both large and small earthquakes.

Sometimes, the edges of plates lock together. They press tighter and tighter against each other. Pressure builds until the plates shift along a fault. This shift causes an earthquake. In an earthquake beneath the ocean, the shifting plates can create a huge wave called a **tsunami** (soo-NAH-mee). Tsunamis can be far more destructive than earthquakes.

In 2011, a powerful underwater earthquake in Japan produced tsunamis that slammed the coast. Giant waves wiped out towns and killed thousands. They also damaged nuclear power plants, causing the release of **radiation**. Japan is still recovering from the disaster.

Tokyo, Japan In 2011, a powerful tsunami toppled many homes and businesses on the coast of Japan.

Northridge, California Earthquakes can cause tremendous damage. A powerful earthquake destroyed thousands of buildings in Southern California in 1994.

Check In What is the Ring of Fire, and where is it?

Let's Hit the Road!

by Grant Herbek

I started this blog to document my family's California road trip. We started near Big Sur and then visited Point Lobos, Monterey, and Pacific Grove. The next day we drove to San Francisco and crossed the Golden Gate Bridge to see Muir Woods. Finally, we drove to gold country. My little brother, Will, couldn't wait to strike it rich. (Yeah, right.)

On the way to Big Sur, I was lucky not to get carsick as we drove on the twisty highway. Hundreds of feet below us, waves crashed against jagged rocks. No sandy beaches there! And definitely no surfing for a beginner like me.

> At Point Lobos State Reserve, ocean waves carved strange shapes and swirls into this sandstone. It looks soft, like regular sand, but it is hard and rough like stone. We climbed all over it.

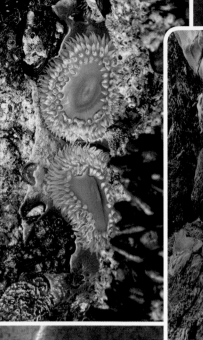

At Big Sur, the waves kept filling this tide pool with water while we checked it out. There were hermit crabs, starfish, and anemones, which look like plants.

Point Lobos was full of birds. Near a place called Bird Island, Will kept screeching at a black bird called an oystercatcher. It screeched right back at him!

Point Lobos

Near Big Sur, we visited Point Lobos State Reserve. A state reserve is an area that's protected from people who'd develop the land, like miners and builders. Point Lobos used to be called "Point of the Sea Wolves." We didn't find any wolves there, but we did see tons of sea lions. The California coast is full of those gray blobs!

Will kept looking through my binoculars, which was annoying. But then he spotted a water spout in the ocean. Could it be a gray whale? Every year, gray whales **migrate** from Mexico to Alaska and back. Sometimes they stop here, so I thought maybe we'd see them. I grabbed the binoculars, but I was too late. Maybe next time.

Pacific Grove

Next, we drove to Lovers Point Park in the town of Pacific Grove. We walked along the coastline and saw scuba divers suiting up on the beach. They told us that they hoped to see otters, starfish, and maybe even rays, which are really flat fish that are related to sharks. I'd like to scuba dive some day, in warmer water.

The ocean along Pacific Grove was full of kayakers. They paddled in calm **inlets** where the waves were small. Pieces of sea plants called **kelp** had washed up all along the shoreline. It smelled bad. I bet the kayakers got their paddles tangled in it. As we left, the wind picked up and the water got choppy. I hope the paddlers made it in safely!

⌄ We spent a lot of time climbing the rocks in Pacific Grove and Monterey Bay, looking for cool rocks for Will's collection.

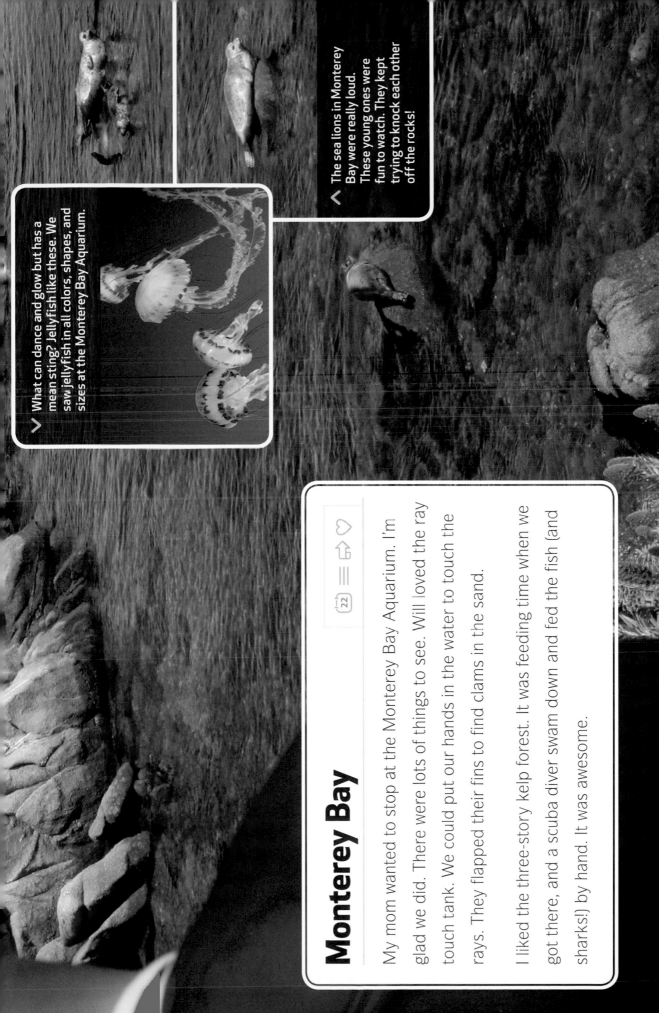

The sea lions in Monterey Bay were really loud. These young ones were fun to watch. They kept trying to knock each other off the rocks!

What can dance and glow but has a mean sting? Jellyfish like these. We saw jellyfish in all colors, shapes, and sizes at the Monterey Bay Aquarium.

Monterey Bay

My mom wanted to stop at the Monterey Bay Aquarium. I'm glad we did. There were lots of things to see. Will loved the ray touch tank. We could put our hands in the water to touch the rays. They flapped their fins to find clams in the sand.

I liked the three-story kelp forest. It was feeding time when we got there, and a scuba diver swam down and fed the fish (and sharks!) by hand. It was awesome.

After an earthquake in 1989, sea lions took over a dock at San Francisco's Pier 39. At one point, more than 1,700 sea lions lived there. It is still home to hundreds of sea lions. It was fun to watch them. There's also a webcam of the sea lions online so you can watch them from home.

It took about four years to build the Golden Gate Bridge. It's more than a mile and a half long.

San Francisco

My favorite part of our road trip was San Francisco. What a city! We did a lot, but I want to go back and do more.

First, we biked across the Golden Gate Bridge. Did you know that it was painted orange so it could be seen in the fog?

Most days it's overcast in San Fran. Luckily, we had a sunny day for our bike ride. After crossing the Golden Gate, we ate lunch in a town called Sausalito. We took a ferryboat back to San Francisco instead of biking eight miles. What a relief. My legs felt like rubber after pedaling up all of those hills. San Francisco is a hilly city!

Alcatraz is an old prison. It was built in the middle of the San Francisco Bay so the prisoners couldn't escape. Alcatraz isn't used as a prison anymore, but you can tour it. We did the spooky night tour. I snapped this picture of the creepy prison hospital. I swear it's haunted.

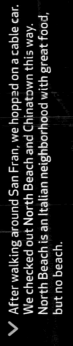

After walking around San Fran, we hopped on a cable car. We checked out North Beach and Chinatown this way. North Beach is an Italian neighborhood with great food, but no beach.

Muir Woods

Muir Woods was named after John Muir. He helped create the U.S. National Park System about 100 years ago. It's a redwood forest 11 miles north of the Golden Gate Bridge.

Muir Woods was incredible. Redwoods stretch up hundreds of feet. Many of these trees are 600 to 800 years old. One is more than 1,200 years old! We did the two-mile hike so we could see a lot of the forest. It was quiet, chilly, and shady.

Coastal redwoods are the tallest living things on Earth. The trees at Muir Woods are around 250 feet tall. Some redwoods grow to be more than 350 feet tall.

> Will must have filled his pan up a thousand times that day. He would shake it left and right so that the heavy gold would move to the bottom.

Gold Country

📅 25 ≡ 🏠 ♡

Finally it was time to let Will pan for gold. We headed toward the mountains. In a few hours, we reached Marshall Gold Discovery State Historic Park in Coloma, California. When we bought some gold pans, the cashier said that a big discovery of gold there helped start the 1849 California gold rush. Will was so excited.

We walked down to the American River. That's where the forty-niners panned long ago. They got their nickname from 1849, the year of the gold rush. We swirled water and sand around in our pans and picked out the gold. Dad said it was probably just pyrite, or "fool's gold." But I didn't tell Will. Striking it rich (sort of) was the perfect end to our road trip.

> My dad loves taking goofy pictures. We couldn't help ourselves when we spotted this tree along the hiking path in Muir Woods.

Check In What's your favorite spot that the blogger wrote about? How would you describe that spot to a friend?

17

SURF'S UP

by Becky Manfredini

In the Hawaiian language, *he'e nalu* means "to ride the waves." That's just what these surfers are doing in Hawaii.

I'm flying. I'm a bird floating on the wind. I'm one with the wave.

This is how many surfers along the Pacific coast describe surfing. They say that "catching a wave" is unlike any other feeling.

Surfing's **origins**, or beginnings, are in Hawaii. In the 1700s, it was considered "the sport of kings." Hawaiian chiefs rode waves to shore on surfboards up to 24 feet long.

Royal Hawaiian boards could weigh up to 175 pounds. They were made of the finest wood. Chiefs would surf the biggest waves to show their courage. In Hawaiian society, **royalty** surfed in their own areas. Regular people could not ride the same waves as royalty.

Surfing Spots

How do surfers find the best waves? They study the direction of the waves and avoid rocky areas. They also look for beaches that aren't crowded. Here are a few favorite surfing beaches:

 Waikiki (WY-kee-kee) Beach is on the Hawaiian island of Oahu (oh-AH-hoo). It's often crowded, but it is a great place for surfing "newbies" to learn.

> Surfrider Beach, in Southern California, became famous after it was in surf films and in songs by a band called the Beach Boys. It's still one of the world's top surfing spots.

The Banzai Pipeline is on Oahu's north shore. Its barrel-shaped waves challenge even the best surfers. Surfers ride through the hollow curl of the wave.

The waves at Mavericks in Half Moon Bay, California, are very tall. They build for a mile before they break, or spill forward. That's when surfers can ride the wave. Each year, Mavericks has a contest where surfers ride dangerous 50-foot waves.

A surfer enjoys an exciting ride at Surfrider Beach in California.

This monster wave is so big they call it Jaws! It can grow as tall as 120 feet. Jaws is located on the Hawaiian island of Maui.

Surfer Gear

What kind of gear do surfers need? It depends. Longboards are very stable. It's easy for beginners to catch a wave on a nine-foot longboard. Shortboards are harder for beginners. Skilled surfers like them, though, because they are easy to handle for performing tricks.

Some people surf without any board. This is called bodysurfing. Bodysurfers paddle through the water with only flippers on their feet. They use their bodies like surfboards.

What about other gear? You'll need only a swimsuit in the warm waters of Hawaii. But in northern California, you'll want to wear a wetsuit. A small amount of water gets trapped under this tight suit. The water warms to your body's temperature. It keeps you warm in cold water.

Long ago, Hawaiians carved boards out of hardwoods such as mahogany. Today, most surfboards are made of plastic-based materials.

How to Speak Surf

If you're around surfers, you might hear, "Dude, that wave was so *gnarly* that I almost got *rag dolled*!" or "That was *da kine*, but now I need to *chillax*." Many surfers use lots of **slang**.

Do you and your friends use words or share jokes that no one else understands? Surfers are a tight-knit group. They use slang, or made-up words, to describe their experiences. The words are often invented by one person and then spread to the whole community. Here are a few words to get you talking like a real surfer.

Duck Dive
forcing your board underwater, diving beneath a wave, and emerging out the other side

Shaka

a hand gesture in which the fingers are curled, with the thumb and pinky out; used by surfers as a greeting or celebration

Hang Ten

a surfing trick in which the board is steady enough atop the wave that the surfer can hang all ten toes off the nose of the board

Wipeout

falling off the surfboard

Barrel

the hollow tube of a breaking wave

CARVE turning as you ride a wave

CHILLAX a mix between chilling and relaxing

COWABUNGA! an exclamation like "Woo-hoo!" that shows you are having a great time

DA KINE in Hawaiian, this means "the best"

GNARLY cool, even beyond extreme or radical

RAG DOLLED to get thrown or tumbled around by a wave

SHRED to do multiple turns on a shortboard

Check In How are shortboards different from longboards, and why would surfers prefer one over the other?

GENRE Social Studies Article

Read to find out | about the eruption of Mount St. Helens and its effects.

A SLEEPING GIANT

A scientist observes a bulge on part of the mountain about a month before the eruption. Rising magma caused the bulge.

RUMBLE, RATTLE, CRACKLE, BOOM!

Washington's Mount St. Helens was a sleeping giant. The volcano had not erupted in 120 years. Hikers visited the beautiful mountain, and many people lived at its base. The mountain rose

Mount St. Helens is one of 37 volcanoes in the Cascade Mountain range. The Cascades extend more than 700 miles through California, Oregon, Washington, and Canada.

Awakens

by Elizabeth Massie

above forests filled with animals. It was surrounded by sparkling lakes.

But in 1980, earthquakes disturbed Mount St. Helens. Cracks began to form in Earth's crust. Pressure began to build. The volcano was about to blow.

Magma, or melted rock, lurks deep inside a volcano before it erupts. When pressure inside Earth becomes strong enough, this trapped magma can erupt. It turns into **lava** as it reaches Earth's surface. When would Mount St. Helens erupt?

Before May 1980, Mount St. Helens stood 9,677 feet above sea level. The eruption blasted away 1,314 feet of the mountain. This made it shorter and rounder.

A VIOLENT ERUPTION

For two months, steam spurted through cracks in the mountain's surface. A bulge appeared on the mountain as magma rose inside. The pressure was building. State police tried to evacuate everyone from the area, but some people refused.

On May 18, 1980, an earthquake triggered a landslide along the north side of the mountain. Then a blast blew that side off. This exposed the magma and uncorked all that pressure. Ash, gases, rocks, and steam shot out at about 300 miles per hour.

A landslide swept down the mountain. Hot rocks and ash rained down on the forests and lakes. Ash darkened the sky 250 miles away.

The earthquake triggers a landslide. This allows explosive gases and magma to escape from the volcano.

Landslides and explosions continue as the side of the volcano blows off.

Less than a minute after the landslide, the sky fills with hot gases and billowing clouds of ash.

The eruption killed 57 people and destroyed more than 200 homes. Lava, ash, and mud buried about 200 square miles of land. Animals and plants were burned. Trees were knocked flat.

"It quickly became as dark as night, yet it was still early afternoon," recalled one local resident. "Even in the short dash from the car to the house, the hot gusts of ash plastered our hair, skin, and clothes with gritty, gray particles."

Rowe Findley is a writer for *National Geographic*. "As soon as I can," he said, "I get airborne for a better look, and recoil from accepting what I see. The whole top of the mountain is gone."

RISING FROM THE ASH

The blast demolished the forests around Mount St. Helens. More than 30 years later, the **conifers** of the evergreen forests have still not fully recovered.

The first plants to come back to the **devastated** area were wildflowers called prairie lupines. Gradually, other plants and animals returned. "The eruption really caused drastic changes in the forest," said one local scientist.

Mount St. Helens has not entirely calmed down. In September 2004, the mountain erupted again but not as severely as in 1980. Still, the eruption kept producing lava until January 2008. As the lava reached the surface, it cooled and hardened into a dome of rock. When the eruption ended, the dome was 1,500 feet high! Scientists are not sure why the eruptions lasted so long.

∧ Mount St. Helens may look calm in this present-day photograph, but don't be fooled. It is an active volcano and has a destructive history!

Today, the area around Mount St. Helens is home to many animals. Tourists hike around the mountain to see how it has renewed itself. But are they in danger? Since 1980, scientists have studied Mount St. Helens. They hope to be able to predict when it will erupt again and if it is safe to explore the restless giant.

Animals like this golden mantled ground squirrel have returned to the area that was devastated by the volcano.

The first plants to come back to the area were wildflowers like these.

Check In Explain how the 2004–2008 eruption of Mount St. Helens differed from the 1980 eruption.

Discuss

1. What connections can you make among the five selections in this book? How do you think the selections are related?

2. Why are there so many earthquakes and volcanic eruptions in the area known as the Ring of Fire?

3. "Let's Hit the Road!" is a firsthand account of a trip to the Pacific coast. How is reading a travel blog different from reading information in your textbook?

4. What are some of the dangers of surfing? What do you think the benefits might be?

5. What else would you like to know about the Pacific coast? How can you find out more about this region?